52 Weeks of Ins[piration]

From The

Animal, Plant & Mineral Kingdoms

For Healing & Harmony

By: Joanne Copley-Nigro, Ph.D.

"Dedicated to those whom I love: my Human and Animal Companions, Teachers who have helped me on my spiritual path, my Spirit Guides and the Message Bringers of the animal, plant and mineral world who inspire me with their beauty and knowledge each day"

About the Author:

Joanne Copley-Nigro is an ordained Spiritualist, Interfaith and Melchizedek Minister with a Ph.D. in Healtheology from the American Institute of Holistic Theology and a B.S.in Occupational Therapy. Joanne is a Reiki Master, Hypnotherapist and Spiritual Pet Healer. She is an active board member for the Church of the Living Spirit and City of Light Spiritualist Church and coordinates many fund raising events. She also serves as a year round Healer at the Healing Temple and is the Lily Dale Volunteer Fire Company's Chaplain. Joanne conducts the annual Blessing of the Animals and Pet Remembrance Service at the Pet Cemetery in Lily Dale.

Her hobbies include gardening, photography and creating Health and Well Being Jewelry, personal gemstone Prayer-Affirmation Beads and Pet Wellness Healing Pendants using natural stones, crystals and shells infused with Healing Reiki Energy.

Contents:

Introduction

INTRODUCTION

"If we could see the miracle of a single flower clearly our whole life would change." Buddha

"Live a life which is an example to others." Djwal Khul (The Tibetan)

"Never limit your view of life by any past experience." Ernest Holmes

"Our prime purpose in this life is to help others. And if you can't help them, at least don't hurt them." Dalai Lama XIV

Be grateful whoever comes because each guest has been sent as a guide from beyond." Rumi

"The Art of Medicine consists of amusing the patient while Nature cures the disease." Voltaire

"Until he extends the circle of compassion to all living things man himself will not find peace. We must be the change we want to see in the world. The greatness of a nation and its moral progress can be judged by the way its animals are treated." Gandhi

"Not to hurt our humble brethren (the animals) is our first duty to them, but to stop there is not enough. We have a higher mission - to be of service to them whenever they require it. If you have men who will exclude any of God's creatures from the shelter of compassion and pity, you will have men who will deal likewise with their fellow men."
Saint Francis of Assisi

"Everything in the world has a hidden meaning… men, animals, trees, stars, they are all hieroglyphics. When you see them you do not understand them. You think they are only men, animals, trees, stars. It is only years later…that you understand." Nikos Kazantzakis

The intention of this book is to reintroduce you to the gifts and messages nature has for your discovery. Every creature, plant and mineral was created by the God of your understanding and contains the unifying life force energy. Everything that exists is connected by this spiritual energy matrix. Whatever happens to one will have an effect on all. Spirit is in all life and all life is spirit. Let us continue in our lives to have reverence for all life and nature and it will help us gain the knowledge we need for spiritual unfoldment. It may be necessary to look closer at that which is all around us in order to understand the symbols and messages that nature brings forth to those who are attuned.

We all have animal allies, plant allies and those also from the mineral kingdom that are here to empower us in our spiritual growth and healing. I am just a voice who carries the words that have been spoken for eternity. I hope these words will connect you with the divine in realizing your relationship with all that is. May these words inspire you and bring personal meaning for you on your life path.

No one could ever give all the recognition each that each animal, plant or mineral on this earth deserves. It is up to you to look, learn, explore and open your heart to the messages that are there for you. When you are meditating on each of the weeks, look deeper into what this animal, plant and mineral is saying to you. Pay attention to each detail, each feather, fur and fin, petal, leaf and color. The characteristics described may just be the beginning point for your personal message to emerge.

Each animal, plant and mineral has a message of its own and each message is unique for those who seek it. When I look into the eyes of an animal I see the eyes of God and I feel connected to their heart space. For that instant there is a subtle communication that takes place where we both know we are one.

When I look at the plant kingdom I give reverence for their service to the earth in maintaining our atmosphere which supports all life. When I look at the mineral kingdom I am transformed into the past and future sharing in an energy grid that is omnipresent in all things.

Let each message bringer in nature bring you the impressions and inspiration that is needed by you. After receiving this knowledge and healing give thanks for all that has been given. Your gratitude in words and actions should always be offered to gift Mother Earth.

Learn each day from your meditation and experience, being mindful of all your impressions, thoughts, words and actions. Generate acts of love, kindness and wisdom from your transforming consciousness. Think, feel and do something good each day for your good and the good of others.

Our purpose for being on earth is for spiritual development and soul growth. This can be achieved by loving other humans, our animal brothers and sisters, the plants, mineral kingdom and all of nature. For every soul, every entity, everything is energy and is interconnected. We can create peace, love, happiness and health in our lives and continue to expand these positive aspects out to manifest in the world. Be grateful for the amazing manifestations of Spirit that serendipitously appear in your life.

Our attitudes affect our health because the body becomes what the mind believes. What you think of continually will eventually become. May this book be a reminder for you to further your exploration in the beauty, the wonder and the messages that nature has for you. It is well established that there is a mind-body connection and that the mind plays an important role in healing. A favorite quote of mine by the philosopher Voltaire is, "The Art of Medicine consists of amusing the patient while Nature cures the disease."

In Buddhism there is a saying that states, "Resolve yourself. It's not just by sitting with your eyes closed that you develop wisdom. Eyes, ears, nose, body and mind are constantly with us, so be constantly alert. Seeing the trees, animals & rocks can all be occasions for study. Bring it all inwards. See clearly within your own heart. If some sensation makes an impact on the heart, witness it clearly for yourself, don't simply disregard it."

Animals are our Companions, Allies, Teachers, Guides, Guardians and Message Bringers. They are the powerful bridges to the world of Spirit. Since time immemorial humans believed that they could speak freely with the natural world and that the Divine could speak with them through Nature. I believe that spirituality is gained from random acts of kindness that promote love & compassion for all beings. Bless the creator of all, the universe, all beings in it and most of all bless you.

These questions can apply to any of the Animal, Plant or Mineral (APM) Kingdoms that you may encounter.

Questions to ask with each weeks lesson and meditation:

- What is this APM trying to show me?
- How does the APM make me feel?
- What emotions does it elicit?
- What attracts me to this APM?
- What have I overlooked in myself that this APM reminds me of?
- This APM maybe a symbol of your qualities and abilities.
- It may reflect on situations that you need to be aware of.
- It may represent obstacles that you need to overcome in your life.

Keep a journal and make note of your experiences in nature.

Sometimes the message in not clear at the time of the encounter but will have far greater meaning at a later time.

Look about you; take hold of the things that are here. Let them talk to you, learn to talk to them. "Nature is an unlimited broadcasting station through which God speaks if we tune in." George Washington Carver

As you reconnect with your animal allies, plant allies and those from the mineral kingdom give thanks for the spiritual growth and healing they have brought into your life. Let us live our lives with reverence for the great things that God has created. I hope this book will bring you knowledge, health, happiness and joy as you travel your life path.

Love and Blessings

Week One
Empathy and Healing

ARMADILLO represents empathy, personal protection and sensitivity. They are the only animal besides humans that can get leprosy and were influential in discovery of a vaccine. Females give birth to 4 identical babies and the young are born with soft leathery skin that hardens in a few days. Their armor is their main defense and protection, although usually they will flee from predators. Known to move quickly and when startled jump straight up in the air. They are also swimmers and hold their breath to walk under the water.

ALOE has been called the "medicine plant" and is about 96% water. The sap is considered to have healing qualities and used for centuries by various cultures for medicine and cosmetics. Aloe was also thought to bring peace to the grieving by the Ancient Egyptians and Greeks. Also believed that it is good for protection in the home, assists with preventing household mishaps and can bring good luck.

AGATE said to foster love, protection, an appreciation of nature and soothing emotions. It strengthens the intellect and the body's physical energy field. In ancient times it was valued as an amulet to quench thirst, protection from fevers and divert storms. It provides balance between mind, body and spirit and improves concentration and memory. It promotes goodwill, allows one to set boundaries and alleviates hostility.

I am compassionate to all beings that need healing.

Week Two
Joy and Energy

HUMMINGBIRD is the symbol of joy, energy, hope and life's sweetness. Humming birds have the highest metabolism of any warm blooded animal and must consistently consume nectar from preferably red flowers to stay alive. They are persistent and migrate sometimes flying as far as 2000 miles to reach their destination. The hummingbird brings beauty and jubilation.

PANSY is a symbol of merriment, cheer, remembrance of those in spirit and, kindheartedness. Pansy is a type of violet, taken from the French word "panse" meaning romantic thought. Thought to have magical love powers and even mend broken hearts. German legend relates people came from miles around to smell the flower and by doing this destroyed the grass around the pansies making it difficult to feed their cattle. So God took the scent away, but gave it great beauty instead.

RHODONITE is a dark and light pink stone good for the heart chakra. It allows you to see joy and love in life's experiences and release the past. Strengthens your resolve, helps express confidence and lovingness on the physical plane. It heightens interest in daily activities bringing out the beauty of life. Helps attunement, spirituality, increases love potential, dispels stress and said to enhance feelings of hope and brotherhood.

I am open for more joy and prosperity to unfold in my life and I will share this with others.

Week Three

Independence and Clear Perception

CAT symbolizes independence, mystery, magic, cleverness and curiosity. The cat teaches be true to your own nature and use clear perception. Follow your intuition and gain understanding from your own internal wisdom. Sometimes the best cure for a problem is to step away from it. Cats are associated with the mystery of the dark and are proficient in balance and hunting, because of the greater number of rods in the retinas of their eyes. Seen as the guardians of the "other world" and are Familiars to witches and wizards. In Ancient Egypt considered goddesses and associated with fertility in Scandinavian lore.

WLLOW is said to release all sadness, is often associated with magic, night visions and lunar rhythms. It has a long history of symbolism associated with metaphysical and ritualistic practices and is used in ceremonies to enhance psychic abilities. Said to be able to bring peaceful healing to body and mind.

TIGERSEYE is a yellow golden brown banded stone used for the Solar Plexus Chakra. It was used in protective medicine by the Roman soldiers during battle. It is said to represent the sun and earth and brings optimism, personal power, grounding and balancing. It will also assist to stimulate intuition and enhance awareness and perception.

I am true to my nature and create a life that is beneficial to me and all others.

Week Four
Loyalty and Service

DOG symbolizes loyalty, companionship and devotion. One of dog's greatest attributes is the capacity for unconditional love. They have long served as a guardian, loyal companion and have provided loving service beside humans since time immemorial as evidenced in primitive cave art. They are infinitely faithful and committed to loving kindness, assistance and protection.

IRIS has the meaning of forthrightness. The three leaves of the iris represent faith, wisdom, and valor. The Greek word Iris means rainbow. The flower got its name from the Greek goddess Iris, the goddess of the rainbow, who was a messenger on Mount Olympus. Iris would take messages from the eye of Heaven to earth by the arc of the rainbow. It was used by Ancient Greek Physicians with honey for healing many types of physical disorders.

SAPPHIRE is a blue stone good for the throat chakra and in Greek means "true blue" This gemstone's legend has it that it is the stone of fidelity. Said to heal, enhance mental clarity, provide protection and is the symbol of heaven. Many kings throughout history are said to have worn Sapphire to protect them from the harm of battle or as an antidote against the effects of poison. In India people believe it to be a symbol of truth and loyalty.

I am grateful for the blessings in my life and lovingly share my abundance with others.

Week Five
Resourcefulness and Balance

SQUIRREL symbolizes resourcefulness, planning, balance of work and play, preparedness and socialization. Known to prepare for the future by burying seeds and nuts, only recovering a small percentage; however it is important since they gift earth with new plant and tree growth. They are social animals, learn through imitation, are extremely observant and communicate vocally and with flicks of their tail. They appear in the art of Ancient Mayan Ruins representing the need for the storage of grain for the people.

DANDELION symbolizes perseverance, known as the message carrier and represents tenaciousness. It is a plant that is prevalent everywhere in the Northern Hemisphere. They are entirely edible and have more beta carotene than carrots, more iron than spinach and are used medicinally for a number of conditions. They are resourceful in propagating by seeds blown in the wind.

GREEN JADE is a green stone good for the heart chakra and symbolizes balance, abundance, resourcefulness and wealth. It has been especially revered among Ancient Mayan and in Chinese and Southeast Asian cultures where it is commonly kept for ensuring health, prosperous life and bringing good luck. Belief is that it becomes greener over time absorbing sickness from the body.

**Anything I can imagine can be achieved,
when it is for the greater good of all.**

Week Six

Introspection and Timing

BEAR symbolizes intuition with instinct, introspection and awareness to timing. Bears mate in the summer and hibernate in dens during the winter without food, drink or relieving themselves for 3-5 months. Mothers waken to give birth at the correct time, when her fat reserves and milk production are ready. Bears are not violent and rarely attack other animals or humans except when surprised, protecting young, eating or if there is a territorial dispute. Bears' wisdom is about timing and preparation.

ELM TREE symbolizes strength of will and intuition. Elm wood is valued for its interlocking grain, and consequent resistance to splitting, thus used for certain kinds of carpentry with significant uses in wheels, chair seats and coffins. It has a distinctive canopy of leaves which grows well in cities producing shade. A homoeopathic tincture is made of the inner bark, and used as an astringent.

LABRADORITE is an iridescent blue-gray-green stone good for the Third Eye and Crown Chakra symbolizing transformation, intuition, introspection and self knowing, especially during times of conflict and change. It is used to bring balance in life, allows one to understand their destiny and assists with dream recall.

The rhythm of life unfolds and I follow my divine life path as it is revealed to me.

Week Seven

Tranquility, Calmness and Meditation

KOALA symbolizes calmness, living in the present moment, tranquility and meditation. They are not a bear but a marsupial, carrying their young in a pouch until maturity. They have underactive adrenals making their metabolism very slow, making them very passive and are known to sleep up to 20 hours a day. They eat predominantly eucalyptus leaf, and hardly drink. They are focused despite being so relaxed.

LAVEVDER symbolizes a sense of calm and tranquility. As an essential oil is one of the most popular and well-known calming scents available. It is said to relax mind and body, helpful to ease insomnia and diffuse stress and anger. The plant originated in the Arabia and India, and was introduced to English gardens in the 1500s. Lavender is derived from the Latin word lavo, meaning "to wash," and this reflects the plant oil's common use in soaps and cosmetics.

LEPIDOLITE is a lavender-rose colored stone good for the Third Eye and used to help with relieving stress. Said to bring calmness and relaxation and because it is a lithium-mica stone is useful for mood swings and sleep. Historical spiritual lore states it was used for menopause and soothing the body. If placed by computers it will clear electromagnetic pollution which causes computer stress in people.

I am centered, balanced and grounded in awareness of Spirit as I meditate each day.

Week Eight
Love and Passion

DOVE is a symbol of love, peace and spirit in many religions. Doves' pair bond for life, if one should die the other will remain solitary. The early Greeks and Romans believed doves represented devotion and family. Said to be the sacred bird of Aphrodite and Venus and a representation of love at weddings and anniversaries.

ROSE symbolizes love, romance, beauty and devotion. They are one of the most admired flowers for beauty and fragrance and are used in cosmetics, aroma therapy and in medicinal remedies. Throughout history have been symbolic of love, passion and commitment. Ancient Greeks and Romans associated roses with Aphrodite and Venus, goddesses of love. Used for hundreds of years to convey love messages without words. Cleopatra spread rose petals around her bedroom chambers.

ROSE QUARTZ is a pink stone good for the Heart Chakra and represents love, compassion and harmony. It has historically believed to bring and restore love, youthful qualities and self-esteem. It promotes joy of each new day and helps one appreciate beauty in people and things. It adds positive love energy to relationships and homes.

**Discover your love, live life with passion
and then share this with the world.**

Week Nine
Illusion and Self Realization

DRAGONFLY symbolizes illusion, dreamtime and self realization. They represent change that takes place for a deeper meaning of life. The word Dragonfly has its source in the myth that they were once dragons. They have been around for almost 300 million years and are very agile and can fly at speed of 35mph and moving in all six directions. Its wings and body are iridescent and it appears to be different colors depending on the light falling upon it. The property of iridescence is associated self discovery and removal of inhibitions.

LOTUS symbolizes intellect, mental energies and illumination. It grows in muddy water to the clean surface and blooms into a flower of beauty. It is a symbol of complete enlightenment and inspires with its unique growth pattern in Buddhism, Egyptian and Thai traditions. It will bloom in several colors, including orange, yellow, white, pink, blue and red. It is also used in various food recipes, medicines and in perfumes.

AMETHYST is a purple/indigo colored stone for the Third Eye and Crown Chakra. It is a physical representative of the Violet Ray. It enhances spiritual awareness, inspiration, balance, psychic abilities, inner peace, imagery, mind quieting and positive transformation. It increases activity in right brain, cuttings through illusion to develop psychic abilities and channeling. It has been called the stone of transformation or metamorphosis.

**With spiritual intuition
I can see clearly and completely.**

Week Ten

Gentleness and Innocence

DEER symbolize gentleness, sensitivity and innocence. Deer are seen with religious figures depicting peace such as St. Francis and Buddha whose first teaching were at the Deer Park in India. Native Americans believed deer could provide knowledge of pharmacology of plants. They are found around the world and native to all continents except for Australia and Antarctica. Fawns are protected by their lack of scent and mother deer keeps them hidden in bushes checking up on them many times a day to feed them. Young deer stay with their mothers for 1-2 years. Deer are herbivores and threaten no other animal.

LILY OF THE VALLEY symbolizes sweetness, sensitivity and innocence. It is a fragrant flowering ground cover that loves shade. It has been used in religious ceremonies and in gardens around the world. It was known as the May Lily and represents purity, happiness and humility. All parts of the plant are considered poisonous if ingested.

CALCITE represents purification, peace, calming, awareness and the appreciation of nature. Calcite comes in white, blue, pink and all are helpful in reducing stress and producing calmness and gentle thoughts. Calcite is probably the premier cleanser of stored negative energy on the physical, emotional and etheric planes and is said to be a purifying stone. It also promotes creativity and imagination and vibrancy.

I hold the vision of calmness and peace for all beings.

Week Eleven
Courage and Valor

LION symbolizes leadership, personal power, strength, royalty and courage. Known as the "King of the Beasts" and as a sign of majesty for many centuries. Their image is seen guarding temples, bridges and tombs with loyalty, power and grandeur. In Ancient Greece they are seen drawing the chariots for the gods and goddesses and are also seen as the ultimate protectors of hearth and home. The male guards the territory and cubs and females are the primary hunters for the pride.

OAK symbolizes bravery, strength, magnificence, luck and represents the tree of life. There is much lore throughout history recognizing and honoring the magnificent oak. They are known to surpass 200 years of age making it a representation of stability and nobility. Socrates regarded the Oak Tree as an oracle tree and the Druids believed the leaves of this tree had the power to give strength and healing.

AQUAMARINE is a pale greenish-blue stone good for the Heart Chakra and Throat Chakra. It symbolizes courage and its flowing vibration helps with calming your emotions and allows you to lead a more noble life in communication with the Divine source of all that is. There are Greek and Roman myths that tell of Aquamarine coming from the treasure chests of mermaids. Historically those that traveled by sea wore aquamarine for courage, protection and for prosperous journeys.

I am courageous and I can accomplish what I desire.

Week Twelve
Individuality and Community

ZEBRA symbolizes maintaining your individuality within the herd. Its black and white stripes provide camouflage against predators; however their patterns are unique for each individual zebra. They have keen hearing and smell and are highly sensitive to smoke. Zebras communicate with facial expressions and sounds and are supportive to one another since they can only sleep when there is another member of the herd right next to them, awake and on guard.

ASH TREE symbolizes how inner and outer worlds are linked, as in the macrocosm and microcosm. They represent sacrifice, sensitivity and higher awareness. The wood is white, strong, straight-grained and is used for baseball bats, tool handles, furniture and flooring. Ash is a large deciduous tree with smooth, gray bark on young trees which becomes fissured with age. The leaves are green above, white below, and turn yellow, red, or purple in the fall.

CITRINE is a yellow-light orange stone good for the Solar Plexus. It symbolizes individuality, confidence, determination, logic and the intellect. The name citrine comes from the Latin word citrus, meaning "*lemon*." As a gemstone for healing for almost 6000 years it is said to be good for relationships, smoothing family or group problems and assists with public speaking and communicating in groups.

I feel harmony and satisfaction in all my relationships.

Week Thirteen
Ancient Knowledge and Purpose

ELEPHANT symbolizes past life knowledge, ancient powers, good luck, strength and caring for yourself and others. Elephants live for 60-70 years and are honored for their family devotion. They are extremely intelligent and have memories spanning many years. They can communicate over distances by producing a sub-sonic rumble traveling across the ground so other elephants may receive this message through the sensitive skin on their feet and trunks. Touching is an important part of their communication and they display grief, joy, anger and play.

REDWOOD TREE is a symbol of forever, great teacher of ancient wisdom. They are the tallest trees on the earth, some reaching 350 feet tall. These trees can live 2000 years and weigh upwards of 500 tons. As they grow upwards they usually lose their lower limbs, producing a canopy over the forest. One of the keys to the survival of the redwood is its regenerative ability.

LAPIS LAZULI is a dark blue-indigo stone with flecks of gold used by the Ancient Egyptians to access sacred knowledge. It symbolizes perfection. It is a stone good for the Throat Chakra and Third Eye. It provides cleansing of mind, body and spirit of negativity. Known universally as a stone to assist with spiritual development.

I contemplate and understand the eternal oneness with all beings great and small.

Week Fourteen
Guidance, Learning and Relationships

WOLF symbolizes spirit teaching, learning, guidance and the importance of social relationships. It has been the grand teacher for many Native Americans. The wolf has been misunderstood and misrepresented in fairy tales as a vicious villain when in fact they are shy, but very sociable among their own species with strict social order and are highly communicative within the pack.

HAZEL NUT TREE symbolizes the ability to discover hidden wisdom in a unique manner and its name indicates the quality of "quiet spirit". From ancient times it was used for the manufacture of wands and royal scepters. Hazel nuts were believed to heighten ones awareness for learning. The hazel nut is a good source of protein and omega fats allowing them to provide nourishment for brain function. The hazel nut tree alerts us to act upon our insights if we wish to transform our life.

SODALITE is a blue and white stone good for the Throat Chakra. It is helpful for learning and all types of communication. Ancient truth seekers relied on stone to call out their inner truths. It assists with deeper thinking, logic and efficiency. It also supports fellowship, ending arguments and brings out truthfulness.

Express your truth and take control to follow your unique path in life.

Week Fifteen
Tranquility and Autonomy

PANDA represents tranquility and self sufficiency. Chinese legend is that a panda discovered a girl had died saving a panda from a leopard and in gratitude the panda held a funeral for her. The pandas wept for the girl and rubbed their eyes on their black arm bands of mourning, thus staining their eyes forever. The panda symbolizes the Yin and Yang and represents peace and harmony. The panda is 99% herbivore, eating 20-30 lbs of bamboo a day. In the wild they conserve their energy by rarely competing for food, territory or mates.

BONSAI TREE symbolizes tranquility, peace, balance and all that is good. The cultivation of bonsai trees originated in China and later with Zen Buddhist Monks in Japan where these miniature trees were pruned into various unique shapes.

FLUORITE is a translucent light purple/green stone good for the Third Eye Chakra which promotes harmony and peace. Its colors are good for auric cleansing, balance, healing, heightening physic energy and inter-dimensional communication with Nature Spirits. Fluorite is excellent for clarity of mind, objectivity, concentration, meditation.

I am at peace with myself and all that is centered in the awareness of Spirit.

Week Sixteen
Purification and New Beginnings

FROG symbolizes purification, rebirth, renewal and metamorphosis. In Egypt frog-headed Heket is the sacred midwife of birthing. Ancient Celts believed frogs had a curative power because of their connection with water. In China the frog is representative of Yin energy and bringer of good luck. They are an amphibian, meaning "two-lives" since they begin their life as an egg in water, then tadpole until metamorphoses into an adult frog living on land and in water.

DAFFODIL symbolizes rebirth, new beginnings, renewed energy and sunshine. This flower is also known as Narcissus and is native to meadows and woods. The daffodil is a multi-purpose flower representative of spring time and new beginnings. They are poisonous if consumed but the bulbs are used medicinally help relieve pain, heal wounds, burns and scars.

BLACK TOURMALINE is a black stone good for the Root Chakra. It is said to be of purifying, cleansing and is a talisman of protection. This stone is said to dispel environmental pollutants, electromagnetic smog, and radiation from cell phones, computers, and other electronic equipment turning the negative energy forces into positive usable energy. It is also good for cleansing the emotional body of negative thoughts, anxieties and anger.

I am cleansed of the past and look to the light within to prepare for new beginnings.

Week Seventeen
Abundance and Prayer

BUFFALO symbolizes manifesting abundance through right action and prayer. Native Americans revere the buffalo as one of the most sacred animals. Desires can be manifested by right thoughts and prayers. Buffalos weigh up to a ton and have a humped shoulder representing storage of forces to be utilized for future need.

CHRYSANTHEMUM symbolizes abundance, wealth, cheerfulness, optimism and truth. The name is derived from the feminine form of Greek Chrysanthos, meaning "golden flower." Buddhists use this flower as offerings on alters as an attractant of good luck. In China the petals are eaten in salads to increase longevity.

BLOODSTONE symbolizes generosity, courage, vitality and health. It is a stone that is a dark green with bright red spots of iron oxide and is good for the Sacral Chakra. Bloodstone helps center and ground oneself. It is believed to prolong life and assist in acquiring wealth. It helps with courage and brings mystical energies of increasing adaptability and organization. It has been used for clearing and mobilizing blockages for attainment of homeostasis.

**My inheritance is abundance, as I give freely,
it is multiplied for my receiving.**

Week Eighteen
Fertility and New Ideas

  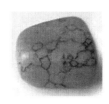

RABBITT symbolizes fertility, new ideas and the release of fear or defeat. The rabbit also appears in folklore as a trickster using slyness to outwit his enemies. In Roman times, the white rabbit symbolized love and sexuality. It was believed that the rabbit was the pet of the Goddess of love, Aphrodite. Rabbits are not rodents but belong to the order called lagomorphs. Rabbits are very intelligent, curious, loving animals with a life span of 8-12 for pets and 1-3 years in the wild.

CACAO TREE symbolizes fertility and life. The Mayans believed that the gods found the cacao tree and gave it to man as a present. It is used in food, drinks, rituals and even as a form of currency in Mayan and Aztec cultures. The cocoa bean contains phenyl ethylamine, "the love chemical", serotonin, which is depression preventing, tryptophan which is relaxing and pain relieving and nature's endorphin: anandamine, as well as vitamin A, B, E and C.

CHRYSOPRASE is an apple green opalescent stone good for the Heart Chakra. It was used by the Ancient Greeks, Romans, and Egyptians in jewelry for spiritual protection and to increase fertility. This stone balances between male and female energies, stabilizes hormones and promotes love for oneself and others.

Discover something new each day and fertilize these new ideas into goals.

Week Nineteen
Dreams and Emotions

SWAN symbolically is representative of transformation, dreams, wonder and love. Swans are close relatives to geese and ducks. They are often a symbol of love because of their monogamous relationships with their partners for life. In fairy tales they remind us of how the ugly duckling was transformed into a graceful swan. In the Vedic literature a person who has attained great spiritual capabilities is sometimes called a Paramahamsa or "Great Swan". In Lily Dale the swan is a symbol of Spiritualism as is the Sunflower.

SUNFLOWER has a symbolism associated with Adoration and Spiritualism. Sunflowers turn their heads to the sun as Spiritualists turn toward the Light of the Divine. Legend of the Sunflower shows it represents life as they have seven branches, (seven days in a week), twelve leaves, (twelve months in a year), 52 yellow petals, (52 weeks in a year) and each flower has 365 seeds (365 days in a year).

OPAL is an opaque white with various colored flecks stone and is good for the Heart and Crown chakra. The stone is made of 30 percent water and is said to help one understand the mystic elements of life. It is a stone associated with emotions, dreams, love, visualization and imagination. The Ancient Egyptians believed opal had a protective power against disease and called it "Gem of the Gods".

Change is a natural way of life in nature.
I am an authentic expression of life.

Week Twenty
Freedom and Movement Forward

HORSE symbolizes freedom, movement, willingness to work and independence. The horse is an animal that is domesticated by humans since 4,000 BC, but has maintained a strong energy and drive of its own. It has contributed more to humanity's advancement than any other animal. In Ancient Greece it was given not only wings but immortality because it was able to recognize its owner and return their love.

BIRD OF PARADISE is a flower symbolizing freedom, good perspective and faithfulness. It originates in South Africa and South America. It is so named because of its resemblance to the actual bird of paradise with long, colorful petals and will grow up to six feet in the wild. This flower has become the focal point of many artists' works with its bright hues and exotic features.

CARNELIAN is a dark orange-red stone good for the Sacral Chakra. It is a stone symbolizing vitality, encourages movement and optimism. Ancient Egyptians carried it as a source of constant renewal and vitality and placed it in tombs as a "magic armor". It is said to encourage healing of open sores, rheumatism, and helps provide more physical energy.

I confidently move forward in my life with energy, health and vitality.

Week Twenty One
Life Force Energy and Exuberance

DOLPHIN symbolizes play, harmony, life force, new creations and dimensions. Dolphins are viewed as free-spirited, providing a connection with one's higher self and are said to be the keeper of the sacred breath of life by Native Americans. The Greeks called them "sacred fish," and killing them was considered sacrilegious. The sun god, Apollo, also assumed the form of a dolphin at Delphi. They are intelligent, use echo-location, are able to understand sign language, generalize information and display altruistic behaviors toward humans.

DELPHINIUM symbolizes fun, lightness, levity and enthusiasm. The name comes from the Greek word "delphis" referring to the flower's resemblance to the bottle-like nose of the dolphin. The flower was used by Native Americans making blue dye and keeping away scorpions.

HEMITITE is a black metallic like stone that is good for the Root Chakra. It is said to eliminate negativity, assist with grounding and balancing the mind-body-spirit connection. It can assist with enhancing mental activity, balance yin/yang energy and emotions. It was used to improve oxygen supply to the body and enhance personal magnetism.

I recognize my personal life force energy and I create joy all around me.

Week Twenty Two
Gentleness, Humility and Self Worth

DONKEY is a symbol of humility, gentleness, patience, peace and stubbornness. They are actually kind natured and eager workers willing to take on the responsibilities and burdens of others but are not receptive to changes. If they feel they cannot do something - they absolutely won't do it, not because of being stubborn but because they listen to their own intuitive senses, knowing their boundaries.

DAISY is a representative of innocence, humility, simplicity, loyalty and purity. Daisies are believed to be more than 4,000 years old and their images were found on Egyptian ceramics and Ancient Greek jewelry. Daisies are said to be durable survivors since they are easy to grow, are versatile in decorating and can be found throughout the world.

HOWLITE is a white stone with grey veining and is good for the Crown Chakra. It symbolizes patience, gentleness, and reasoning. Said to reduce stress, anxiety and absorb your own anger, or another's anger that is directed toward you. It also helps to overcome critical or selfish behaviors bringing a new appreciation of people and self. It is commonly used to make carvings or jewelry and is dyed to imitate other minerals and stones.

I am an authentic expression of life and believe in the good I represent.

Week Twenty Three
Wisdom and Vision

OWL is often seen as a symbol of wisdom, magic, clairvoyance and mystery. Ancient Greeks associated it with Athena, symbolizing higher wisdom. In Ancient Egypt and Hindu culture the owl was a guardian of the underworld. They have been a familiar to witches, wizards and sorcerers in media throughout history. Owl is nocturnal and has acute vision and hearing making it able to see what others cannot.

MARIGOLD represents wisdom, creativity, attracts positive energy and helps dreams come true. Marigolds were used by herbal healers for centuries for medicinal purposes. During the fourteenth century, many believed it had "magical powers." During the Civil War and World War I, marigolds were used to prevent wounds from getting infected. Marigolds originated in Egypt and were first introduced to Britain and other countries by the Romans where it was one of the earliest cultivated flowers, known as the "Herb of the Sun".

AMBER is a golden-yellow color stone good for the Solar Plexus. Amber is technically not a gemstone or mineral, but a fossilized sap from prehistoric trees that has aged over the course of millions of years. It is said to strengthen the intellect and the body's energy field. It is used for energy, heightening clarity of thought and assists with remembrance of past lives and ancient wisdom.

With prayerful reflection I gain insight, guidance and vision.

Week Twenty Four
Prosperity and Generosity

PIG symbolizes generosity, prosperity, wealth, happiness, intelligence and seeing the best in others. They have taken on countless meanings in popular culture and literature. Native Americans recognized the pig as a symbol of the abundance of daily life, teaching us to celebrate life and share it with others. In the 1880's a tradition developed of sharing a peppermint-flavored confection in the shape of a pig after Christmas dinner. It was hoped to bring health and prosperity for the New Year. Pigs are extraordinarily intelligent, the fourth smartest animal on earth. They are social, clean and bond well with other animals.

MONEY TREE is said to bring financial fortune and cause great things to happen. Its botanical name is Pachira Aquatica, a native plant in Mexico, Guyana and Brazil. The five leaves are representative of the five elements of feng shui: metal, wood, water, fire and earth. The leaves, flowers and seeds are all edible.

AVENTURINE is a green stone good for the Heart Chakra. It symbolizes abundance, good luck, and helps us to see all possible alternatives and potentials. It is a stone which enhances prosperity and success yet balances our heart and emotions. Ancient Greek warriors wore aventurine when going to war to prevent injury or death.

I express gratitude for that which I have and share the goodness.

Week Twenty Five
Spiritual Vision and Guidance

EAGLE symbolizes freedom, courage, spiritual power, intelligence and judiciousness. They are seen by Native Americans as a connection to the Great Spirit, the creator of all things. Their sharp vision enables them to see hidden truths and spiritual principles. The eagle allows us to maintain balance and recognize our connection with all life. Bald eagles are monogamous and pairs mate for life. Eagle has been the national emblem of the US since 1782.

CINNAMON TREE symbolizes spirituality, success, healing and psychic development. It is called the "tree of folk healers". It has been dated back to the Ancient Egyptians who used it for rituals, embalming, wound healing and to raise spiritual vibrations and psychic power. The olfactory sense is a powerful tool to help enhance our intuition and intuitiveness. Cinnamon is pleasing and stimulates the senses.

CELESTINE is a light grey-blue stone also known as Celestite, representing the sky and heavens. It is good for the Crown and Throat Chakras. It is said to have come from the star group called the Pleiades and has an uplifting energy that will raise one's awareness, improve one's eyesight and hearing. Its mineral content has been used for centuries in firework and flares.

Spirit guides me and I follow my higher purpose.

Week Twenty Six
Divination and Discernment

CROW symbolizes cunning, imagination, prophecy and knowledge. Native Americans view them as a manipulative trickster. Crows are interchangeable with ravens and believed to be shape shifters. They are intelligent and known to warn and instruct other birds and animals. They are cunning and use mob behavior to get what they are after. They are North Americas largest song bird and often mimic other bird sounds. They are full of the energy that fuels imagination and insight.

ALMOND TREE symbolizes clairvoyance, enlightenment and the stirring of spirit. Almond trees were first grown in Israel, 2000 years ago, where Moses crafted oil lamps in the image of an almond. Van Gogh often painted almond trees in full flowering radiance. It has been said that the tree holds the key to unlock the door to spirit allowing discovery to the answers you seek.

ANGELITE is a light blue stone good for the Throat Chakra. It symbolizes communication, imagination, telepathy and channeling. It is said to be an assist with angelic attunement and promoting understanding. It assists in speaking the truth. It is a useful stone for any spiritual journey that aligns the physical and etheric fields for healing.

**I look to the Divine for guidance
in my spiritual message work.**

Week Twenty Seven
Determination and Building Dreams

BEAVER symbolizes industriousness, ambition, perseverance and practicality. They also symbolize the importance of spending time with family. They are the largest in the rodent family with large incisor teeth. They have a flat tail which serves as a tool needed to build dams to provide deep water areas which protects them against predators. Their lifespan is about 16 years, they take one mate for life and the family units are called colonies which are made up of adults, yearlings and kits.

HOLLYHOCK symbolizes ambition and fruitfulness. It is a member of the mallow family. It is an edible flower used in home remedies and dyes. Their origin is from Asia around the 9th century and became popular during the Victorian Times in British and American gardens. They are flowers upon a stalk that can grow up to 9 feet tall.

BLACK ONYX is a stone good for the Root Chakra. It symbolizes stamina, steadfastness, tenacity and durability. For centuries it was used to repel negative forces and deflect the negativity of others. It is said to assist with entrepreneurs and inventors. It helps release old beliefs and patterns that no longer serve the person.

I am determined to follow my dreams and create the results that I desire.

Week Twenty Eight
Natural Beauty and Perfection

NAUTILUS symbolizes natural beauty, the sacred spiral, perfection and survival. This sea creature is a Cephalopod that has survived over 450 million years, thus referred to as a living fossil. Its shell is a natural example of a logarithmic spiral which grows into larger chambers throughout its life. Cross-section of the shell demonstrates the Golden Mean Spiral (Phi) or Fibonacci Sequence. This spiral is found in human physiology, plants, minerals, animals, energy patterns and weather, reminding us of our evolving journey and inter-connectiveness.

SPIRAL ALOE also known as Aloe Polyphylla, a plant that represents the sacred spiral in its growth. It is an endangered plant found in higher elevations of South Africa. It is rare, beautiful and used for African tribal medicinal and magical purposes.

AMMONITE is an opal like organic stone made of fossilized shells of ammonites, (ancient ancestors of the nautilus). After being buried for an extended length of time, it acquires radiant color formations that hold a vast amount of energy for healing and growth. It is beneficial for all Chakras.

I unfold with each cycle of life discovering new mysteries and connections.

Week Twenty Nine
Transformation and Imagination

BUTTERFLY symbolizes many things to many cultures, including transformation, change, freedom, soul and imagination. When observing the butterfly we can imagine the opportunities to be free but still remember the stages of life getting us to the present. They bring color and lightness to our thoughts and allow us to use our imagination. When there is an abundance of butterflies there is a well balanced eco-system. They are second to bees in pollinating plants and can only fly when their body temperature reaches eighty-five degrees.

LUPINE is purple blue flower growing on sturdy stalks which symbolize imagination. Their name come from "lupinus" meaning "of wolves" referring to the belief that this plant robbed the soil of nutrients. Lupines have a scent of honey and provide the solitary food for the Karner Blue Butterfly's caterpillar.

MALACHITE is a dark green banded stone good for the Heart Chakra. It's has been called "The restorer of life and the mirror of the soul". It assists the body in healing with its color representation of natures spectrum. It assists with freedom from limiting emotions and releases old habit patterns bringing transformation and balance.

Anything you can imagine can be achieved; you can transform your desires into being.

Week Thirty
Power, Passion and Vitality

TIGER symbolizes strength, power, passion, energy, vitality and health in most cultures. The tiger is the largest member of the cat family; it is a nocturnal hunter and lives a solitary live except for the close bond between the mother and her cubs. Sometimes they are associated with the mystical qualities of water since they are swimmers unlike other cats. Their stripe pattern is unique to each cat. They are considered yang energy, hold the balance of cosmic forces and can attract wealth with their golden color according to Chinese myth.

SAGE represents strength and to the Ancients it was a herb associated with immortality, vitality and mental alertness. Sage belongs to the genus Salvia, meaning "to save." Native Americans use it for medicinal purposes and smudging in order to protect spiritual sanctity. Ancient herbalists believed if you drank sage tea you would never grow old.

GARNET is a deep red stone good for the Root Chakra. It symbolizes passion, self confidence, health and said to protect against negative energy. Ancient travelers wore garnets for protection and believed it to illuminate the night. The stone is also useful in attracting success in business.

With health and vitality I accept my personal power to be all I can be.

Week Thirty One
Growth and Healing

SNAKE symbolizes healing, growth, being flexible and shedding the old for new. It is one of the oldest universal symbols found throughout the world representing both good and evil. It represents the Kundalini power to heighten physical and spiritual power and said to be able to transmute negative experiences into positive spiritual lessons. In some cultures they are treated as Gods while others feel they represent death. A snake and staff has symbolized the healing arts for centuries

CEDAR TREE symbolizes healing, cleansing and protection. Cedar trees are found throughout the world and are cited in the Bible. It produces cones and has fragrant reddish wood and it is considered to be purifying by Native Americans. It was used as charcoal during the American Revolution to make gunpowder and its wood for water barrels to keep water pure. Tradition reveals that the unicorn keeps its treasure in boxes made of cedar.

TURQUOISE is a blue green stone known as a master healer and good for the Throat Chakra. This is a sacred stone to Native Americans said to absorb negative energies, enhance intuition and attunes all chakras. It has been used for centuries as one of the oldest protection amulets for strength, protection, healing and connection to the spirit.

I accept myself as healthy, vibrant and alive this day and every day.

Week Thirty Two
Appearance and Identity

RACCOON symbolizes disguise, the nature of masks, dexterity, curiosity and versatility. They are intelligent, fastidious and can manipulate objects very effectively for their own benefit sometimes fitting the role of a masked bandit. They do not hibernate, but will feed heavily in the fall, storing extra fat so they can stay in their burrows through winter. Raccoons are generally nocturnal. They use water to increase tactile sensation in their hands while handling food or objects.

LITHOPS PLANT also known as Living Stone plant symbolizes disguise. It is a type of succulent plant native to South Africa. The name is derived from the Greek word "lithos" meaning stone of which this plant resembles. Their appearance and coloration provide camouflage to avoid being eaten as they blend into their surroundings.

PYRITE is a metallic gold stone helpful for grounding to the earth. The name comes from Greek "pyr" meaning fire. This was because it was found to create sparks when struck against another mineral. It is known as "Fool's Gold" because of its gold like appearance. It is said to enhance will power and the manifestation of objectives.

Listen to your inner voice for it knows what is for your highest good.

Week Thirty Three
Youthfulness in Life

AXOLOYTL symbolizes eternal youthfulness in life. Axolotls are aquatic amphibians that normally mature and reproduce without developing into adult salamanders. This rare trait called neoteny, (they retain larval features throughout life which is the tadpole like dorsal fin, feathery gills and they just get bigger instead of developing lungs to emerge on to land). They are self healing, able to regenerate a lost limb in a period of months. Found only in fresh Lakes of Central Mexico, they are an endangered species due to pollution and scientific research.

PRIMROSE symbolizes early youth, renewal and beauty. The name means "first rose" as it blossoms in early spring. The primrose is associated with beginnings and youthfulness. It was the symbol and sacred flower of Freya, the Norse goddess of first love. Ancient Celtic wisdom cites the primrose as affiliated with the fairy realms.

SUGILITE is a light purple stone good for the Crown Chakra. It is a healing stone that balances mind, body and spirit and aids in general healing. It represents perfection, inspiration, confidence and alleviates negative/destructive emotions. It allows one to follow their dreams in becoming their authentic self.

**I feel youthful and alive as I greet each day
with intention and purpose.**

Week Thirty Four
Time and Longevity

TURTLE or TORTISE symbolizes self reliance, patience, connection to mother earth, longevity and slowing down. Turtles carry their homes on their back; their shells allow many of them to be adaptable to both water and land. Tortoises have long life-spans of 100 years or more. They have a slow metabolism, sleep 16 hours a day and feed on plants. Native Americans and Chinese lore believed the turtle supported the world on its back.

JUNIPER TREE symbolizes peace, strength and longevity. Found on the British Isles it is said to protect one from injury, bring good health and holds healing powers. In Europe the burning of the wood is highly aromatic and in ancient times was used for the ritual purification of temples, to ward off diseases and to aid in clairvoyance. The base of the juniper tree has a spiny exterior making it an excellent hiding spot for small animals.

RIVERSTONE is a smooth neutral colored stone that has been naturally polished by water. It symbolizes the connection between land and water and it is said to absorb the energy produced by water movement. It has a regenerative effect on the body and relieves anxiety. It relieves worry and fear and allows us to move with the flow.

Each day I forgive the past, welcome the future and enjoy the present.

Week Thirty Five
Feminine Energy and Maternal Love

COW symbolizes the connection to the Great Mother Goddess, female energy, contentment, nourishment, maternal love and new birth. In Ancient Egypt, Hathor was a goddess worshipped as a cow-deity and considered the "nourisher" of all things. To Hindus and Buddhists, the symbolism of the cow deals with patience and holiness. Cows have been called the foster mother of the human race because of milk consumption.

CARNATION symbolizes love, feminine energy and motherhood. These flowers were handed out on the first Mothers Day celebration in 1908. They have lasting qualities; that symbolize the purity and strength of motherhood. Their history dates back to ancient Greek and Roman times and is one of the oldest cultivated flowers. It's scientific name dianthus roughly translating to "flower of love". Pink carnations are universally representative of a mother's love.

MOONSTONE is an opalescent colored stone good for the Heart Chakra and Third Eye. It honors the feminine, lunar energy and symbolizes the female goddess. It is said to stimulate the pineal gland and balance hormones. It is a beneficial stone for women and men to open their emotional self. Traditionally it was used as a protection stone for travelers on sea and land.

**I honor and praise the Great Mother Earth
for all her beauty that surrounds me.**

Week Thirty Six
Paternal Energy and Patience

SEAHORSE symbolizes paternal energy, magic, chivalry, courtship and patience. The male seahorse is loyal, mates for life, bears the young and carries them in their pouch. Ancient Greeks and Romans believed the seahorse was an attribute of Poseidon/Neptune and a symbol of strength and power. Ancient Europeans believed that they took the souls of sailors to safety while passing over. Seahorse populations are endangered by habitat destruction and medicinal use.

FERN symbolizes magic, fascination, confidence, patience and the association with the spiritual realms. Ferns do not have seeds or flowers, but reproduce by spores. There are about 12,000 varieties of ferns worldwide. Ferns can be traced to the Mesozoic Era, over 360 million years ago.

JASPER comes in many colors and pattern designs and it is good for all chakras. It balances the yin/yang energy, emotions, is nurturing and stabilizing. It is said to awaken the heart and mind to new ideas and assists with flexibility and openness to others. Historically it was known for magical powers in many cultures.

In an ever changing world I learn to be adaptable and tolerant of all beings.

Week Thirty Seven
Gentleness and Strength

GORILLA symbolizes the importance of gentleness and nobility in the appearance of strength. Often they are misrepresented as being aggressive when actually they are peaceful, have intricate methods of social communication and emotionally bond to their species and others. They manage other members of their group with restraint, compassion and balance and seldom is there aggression or violence used. Their DNA is closely linked to humans and they are able to learn and communicate using sign language.

PEACE LILY symbolizes gentleness and peace. They are said to bring harmony and calmness to conflict, heal negative energy and foster good relationships. They are known for their ability to cleanse the air of harmful toxins from radiation. Peace Lilies are native to Latin American Rain forests.

PERIODOT is an olive or chartreuse green stone good for the Heart Chakra. It symbolizes purity, peace, understanding, openness and acceptance. It is mentioned in many ancient references as chrysolite and was worn for understanding, as a protector against negative emotions and soothing to those with earthly problems.

My inner peace gives me strength to accept and overcome all challenges.

Week Thirty Eight
Scrutiny, Details and Success

MOUSE symbolizes focus on details, persistence and scrutiny. Primarily nocturnal they compensate for poor eyesight with a keen sense of hearing and smell. They are inconspicuous which often protects them from predators. They are persistent, successful, intelligent, clean and well organized in their environment and altruistic to other mice. Their message is to pay attention to the little things which will lead to bigger opportunities.

MOUSE PLANT or Arisarum Proboscideum is a perennial shade loving plant growing in the woodlands of Spain and Italy. It sprouts unusual maroon flowers with a tubular base from bright green leaves resembling a mouse with tail.

APATITE is a dark blue-purple stone good for the Throat Chakra. It is derived from a Greek word meaning "to deceive" because of the variety of colors and formations it has. Said to enhance intellect, focus, learning, clarity of concentration and ideas. It is a learning stone, making clear your purpose in life. Moon rocks are said to contain trace apatite which is composed largely of phosphorus.

Make sound decisions by being aware of all options and possibilities in order to succeed.

Week Thirty Nine
Foresight and Vision

GIRAFFE symbolizes foresight, moving forward, vision and silence. Giraffe's neck is prominent and symbolizes expression and the throat, despite their silent nature. They are calm and are able to graze alongside other herbivores. Each of their spot patterns is unique to each giraffe and serves as a camouflage against trees and shadows. They have two small horns and a third boney prominence under the skin between the eyes which can symbolize use of the third eye for foresight.

AMARYLIS FLOWER symbolizes silence, timidity, love and splendid beauty. It is a striking red flower native to South Africa. It is commonly associated with the holidays. In Greek mythology it is associated with a story about the love between a quiet and shy nymph that fell in love with a shepherd. In Victorian England, the flower symbolized intense pride and beauty due to its height.

FUCHSITE is a green and violet spotted stone good for the Heart Chakra. It connects the heart and mind and the ability to look forward and ground one's self. It is said to assist with providing protection from harmful vibrations as it redirects energy outward. It is good for looking at deeper levels of consciousness and multi-dimensions.

My intuition is guided by my higher self as I go forward each day.

Week Forty
Uniqueness and Infinite Possibilities

PLATYPUS symbolizes infinite possibilities, creativity, non-conformity and dreams. Platypus is a semi aquatic mammal native to Australia with many unique features like egg-laying, duck billed, beaver tailed, otter footed mammal that nourish young with milk. The males have a venomous spur on their hind feet. Platypus is one of the icons of Australia and their message is to dream & create your own.

VENUS FLY TRAP or the Dionaea Muscipula symbolizes uniqueness in the plant kingdom by it being a carnivorous plant able to attract insects inside of its lobe like petals which close upon its prey. If the prey does escape, the trap usually reopens in about 12 hours. As the prey moves within the jaws of this plant it tightens and digests the prey. In the spring, the plant produces delicate white flowers, but only if it is healthy. It is native to North Carolina bogs.

RAINBOW IRON PYRITE is multicolored stone good for all chakras it was recently discovered found along the banks of the Volga River in Russia. It occurs as a fine layer of shimmering miniature crystals that coats a matrix of pyrite. It is said to promote psychic development, improve memory, practicality and strength of will. It is also said to allow the unfoldment of our unique talents.

Each of us holds a unique beauty that contributes to the whole of life.

Week Forty One
Self Respect and Boundaries

SKUNK symbolizes respect, reputation and keeping boundaries. They are respected and feared by all because of their unique method of self protection. They are solitary peaceful creatures that give warning to those around them of the boundaries that need to be maintained. It takes over a week to reproduce its spray after using it four times so they must be sure to use this defense tool prudently.

WASHINGTON HAWTHORN symbolizes respect and boundaries. This tree has beautiful flowers that bloom in the spring that later turn into berries that are relished by small wildlife and birds. The tree also has thorns that provide this as a defensive security hedge. It is native to the eastern and southern portion of the United States.

HEMIMORPHITE is a stone that is a clear turquoise blue stone good for the Throat Chakra. It symbolizes self-esteem, self-respect and may assist in personal growth. It is said to be used for protection from malice and poisoning; and as a amulet for good luck and transformation.

I respect myself knowing that I always put forth my best effort in all I do.

Week Forty Two
Confidence and Balance

LLAMA symbolizes confidence, gentle balance, healing, comforting others and the ability to move over hurdles. Llamas are an intelligent, trusting and a cooperative member of the camel family native to South America. They are gentle loving companion and work animal that requires little water, are able to carry heavy loads and can maneuver difficult mountain paths. They are sociable with people and communicate by making different humming sounds to warn of danger or to express contentment.

CHAMOMILE symbolizes balanced energy in action. It is a daisy like flower that has been used for its beauty and for its medicinal value for centuries. It has been used to relieve stress, heal mouth problems and makes a soothing tea. According to the U.S National Library of Medicine, there is over 100 sickness conditions in which chamomile has been used traditionally as a medicine.

AMETRINE is a clear purple stone which is good for healing. It enhances the Third Eye Chakra. It is said to aid in meditation, relieves tension, disperses negativity, eliminates prejudice; enhances intuition and concentration. It is known for its soothing effect balancing mind, body and spirit. and resolves inner conflicts.

I am confident and balanced as I apply my inner knowing to all situations I encounter each day.

Week Forty Three
Devotion and Playfulness

OTTER symbolizes playfulness, joy, devotion, nurturing and water energy. The otter is a happy, curious, aquatic member of the weasel family known to use tools. They have strong family bonds and are monogamous creatures that mate for life. The female primarily raises the offspring. Otter will often float in groups while eating, resting and sleeping and will hold hands so they do not drift away from others. They have few enemies and are not afraid of humans.

WISTERIA symbolizes playfulness, joy and adventure. This vine bears purple grapelike clusters of fragrant blooms. In the fall the foliage takes on cheery yellow tones. It is an example of nature's playful spontaneity growing abundantly on various walls and trellises. It is said that the movement of the vine devotedly records the memory of its growth adventure.

ANAUDALITE or Aura Quartz is a natural luminescent, rainbow colored quartz that is from India and good for the Heart Chakra. It is said to bring joy and delight to ones being. Its name means "Divine Bliss". Vibrations from the stone bring energy to your heart making it light and loving. A stone that can create happiness and playful energy.

A balance of work and play is necessary for my continual well being and creativity.

Week Forty Four
Inspiration and Intuition

WHALE symbolizes inspiration, intuition, cosmic consciousness and emotional perception. They are sacred to many cultures and associated with compassion and solitude. They are the largest animal in the world 100 feet long and can live as long as humans. They "sleep" by resting one half of their brain while the other half stays awake to make sure the whale breathes by surfacing. They are known for their songs when communicating and use echolocation to maneuver. Their brain function resembles that of humans and apes in that they exhibit social organization, empathy, intuition and affection.

ROWAN TREE or Mountain Ash symbolizes psychic ability, healing, protection, inspiration and power. Rowan means "flame" in describing the beauty of its berries. Native to Europe, Siberia and Western Asia and North America. This tree is said to be helpful with clearing the mind, assist in attunement with nature and play a role in psychic protection. In Celt and Scottish Folk lore it is considered a sacred wood and used for amulets, dowsing, magic and divining rods.

RUTILATED QUARTZ is clear quartz stone with the inclusion of the mineral Rutile through it. This stone is good for the Crown Chakra and can be used to magnify the energy of intention and manifest affirmations. It assists with receiving spiritual inspiration and developing intuitive abilities.

May I gather from my intuition the knowledge I need to grow and succeed in my life.

Week Forty Five
Adaptability and Cleverness

FOX symbolizes cunning, camouflage, adaptability, cleverness and beauty. Fox has appeared in folk lore and literature around the world portrayed at times as a trickster or animal familiar. Some fox have been domesticated as a result of selective breeding done in the USSR. There are over 37species of foxes, who are a member of the canine family and come in various colors red, black, white, silver and grey to camouflage to their environment. Fox are adaptable omnivores and when hunting they demonstrate various antics to show noninterest to their prey.

HOSTAS symbolize adaptability, variety within conformity. They are hardy perennials that emerge in spring from winter dormancy. Originally native to China, Japan and Korea, they were introduced into the U.S.in the early 1800's. There are over 45 species that range in foliage color, shape, texture and size but they are predominantly a shade loving plant that will adapt to some sun shine.

BRONZITE is a greenish brown with metallic bronze glow stone that is good for the Sacral Chakra. It is found in India, China, Brazil, and Russia. It symbolizes adapting to situations and taking control over them. It allows us to be certain on what we want and how to get it. Said to balance the alkalinity and acidity in the body and aid in the transition from one life cycle to another.

Anything I can imagine can be achieved with the help of Spirit.

Week Forty Six
Color Healing and Communication

PARROT symbolizes color healing and communication. There are over 300 species of parrots that live in the Amazon. The Hindu god of love, Kama, took a parrot as a symbol. Their beautiful colors have fascinated humans throughout history as well as their ability to imitate sounds and speech. Many species of parrots will mate for life, as long as 75 years. Parrot feathers are used in many ceremonies and for healing throughout the world.

COLEUS is a multicolored plant in the mint family that symbolizes the healing aspects of color. There are over 150 species of coleus with arrays of color combinations unmatched by any other species. It is found naturally from Africa to Asia, Australia, and the Pacific Islands. It is prized as an ornamental plant and as important traditional Ayurvedic herb that has been a part of Indian medicine for centuries.

TANZANITE is a deep blue-purple color stone good for the Throat Chakra and Crown Chakra. It is said to link the heart and mind giving one the ability to communicate the truth. It has been used for healing by raising the consciousness and promoting compassion. It is also known as blue zoisite and was discovered in Tanzania, Africa.

Each color of the spectrum brings healing to my body, mind and soul.

Week Forty Seven
Devotion and the Sacred

BABOON symbolizes guarding sacred spaces, intelligence, curiosity and devotion to family. They are an Arabian and African old world monkey with a dog-like muzzle, powerful jaws, canine teeth, close-set eyes, thick fur and short tails. In Ancient Egypt they were considered sacred and associated with Thoth the god of wisdom, science and measurement. The Mayans glorified the monkey and baboons as a symbol of knowledge and prophecy.

HENNA PLANT is a small tropical shrub called (*Lawsonia inermis*) that is native to Africa, Asia, and Australia. It is considered a sacred plant because it produces the reddish-brown dye used for tattoos in many cultural ceremonies.

SHIVA LIGHAM STONE is an earth colored banded egg shaped stone naturally formed in the Narmada River in India; it has been used for energizing the Sacral Chakra. It is considered a gift from the god Shiva and is a sacred prayer stone they symbolizing completeness, the sacred energy between male and female into wholeness and fertility. Traditionally were passed down within families.

**My sense of sacredness begins within me
and I extend that sacredness into the world.**

Week Forty Eight
Luck and Power of Belief

CRICKET symbolizes good luck, longevity and good fortune in many cultures of Europe and the Mid East. They also represent the power of your beliefs and the manifestation of your desires. They are known for their chirping song that will cease when someone approaches thus alerting one of potential intruders or an impending storm. They teach us to be practical yet imaginative to acquire our desired outcomes.

SHAMROCK or clover symbolizes prosperity, good fortune and luck. It is an unofficial symbol of Ireland and St Patrick's Day. The shamrock was traditionally used medicinally since it is high in protein and minerals, digestible when boiled and can be made into teas and flour. Clover is found throughout Europe and the US. A four leaf clover is rare and thus a symbol of good luck.

CAT'S EYE/CHRYSOBERYL is a translucent yellowish colored stone that exhibits a floating light reflection that moves as the gem is rotated making it look like a cat's eye, *(chatoyancy)*. It is a good stone for the Solar Plexus Chakra and said to bring good fortune. In Sri Lanka it is considered a powerful gemstone to protect one from negative energy. It is also used for healing and inducing positive energy.

Greatness is your potential; believe you are capable of what you can imagine.

Week Forty Nine
Travel and Vigilance

GOOSE symbolizes migration, flight, new adventures, fidelity, vigilance and loyalty. If one of the geese is injured during the migration journey, another goose will leave the flock to stay with it until it has recovered or expired. They are gifted navigators and fly as a team often relieving and rotating in their flight positions. Historically they have been portrayed as story tellers

CHERRY TREE symbolizes renewal, rejuvenation and new awakenings. It has been called the tree of the heart because of the energy that it brings in allowing one to recognize the true self. In Washington, D.C., in 1912, they were gifted to us by Japan and symbolize "friendship between nations, the renewal of spring and the ephemeral nature of life". The cherry tree was sacred to Apollo and Venus and burned as an incense to demonstrate love.

CLEAR QUARTZ CRYSTAL is good for the Crown Chakra. It is beneficial for manifesting, healing, meditation, protection and channeling. They reflect and store vibrational energy due to the piezoelectric effect. For centuries it was recognized as a "stone of power," bringing energy of the stars into the soul. Said to be used by Ancient Atlantians and Lemurians.

I bless all those who have helped me on my way to where I am at today.

Week Fifty
Humor and Astuteness

COYOTE symbolizes cunning, humor, magic, and a balance between wisdom and folly. They are known by Native Americans as a shape-shifter, transformer and trickster. They teach us to be wary of playing tricks on ourselves and others because of the consequences of our actions affecting all parties. In nature they are adaptable, nocturnal hunters and scavengers that hunt in packs with use of a wide range of vocalizations to communicate. Native only to North America with keen senses adapting them to different habitats.

COLOMBINE symbolizes folly. The columbine flower was derived from the Latin term columba meaning "dove" or "pigeon-like". The symbolism was of foolishness and at the same time it was also considered a symbol of fidelity. It is native to most temperate areas of the world including Europe and North America and their colors range from white, yellow, red, blue, pink and purple hues.

SNOWFLAKE OBSIDIAN is black with faint white speckles and is good for the Sacral Chakra. Said to enable one to see the best of a bad situation by clearing negative and self-defeating thoughts and inspiring one with new ideas. It clears one's thinking, eliminates energy drain and increases psychic sensitivity. It allows one to notice the meaningful synchronicities in life leading to better life decisions.

Generate acts of kindness and wisdom from your transforming consciousness.

Week Fifty One
Spirit and Life Paths

SPIDER symbolizes connection with spirit, feminine energy, creativity and is called the weaver of the fabric of life. An ancient symbol of mystery, power, magic and growth to many cultures around the world. Native Americans call her Grandmother for she is the teacher and protector of esoteric wisdom. They can spin intricate webs of fragile silk that are one of the strongest fibers known.

PRAYER PLANT symbolizes the need to take time and go within to connect to spirit. A plant originating from the tropical rainforests in Central and South America. The botanical name is Marantaceae or Arrowroot. Its leaves are spotted with striking colors and at night it slowly rolls its leaves up, giving it the name prayer plant. They are a low light house plants because of its natural habitat growing underneath the canopy of tropical trees.

BARITE or Barite Rose is a brown stone resembling a flower. It is good for the Crown Chakra and Third Eye. It is a stone that can aid in moving your life in the direction of your spiritual destiny. It strengthens inner vision and enhances dream recall. Barite is found in Britain, Romania, Germany and the US. It has been associated with healing the earth and for Native Americans, in helping warriors cross over into spirit.

Look within and find your spiritual meaning as you follow your life's path.

Week Fifty Two
Foundation and Hidden Meaning

WOMBAT symbolizes digging to find hidden meanings, determination and foundation. They are a shy marsupial that resembles a cute bear with small ears that can hear frequencies and sounds unknown to humans. They inhabit Australia and Tazmania, live a solitary life, dig elaborate burrows and tunnels, are nocturnal herbivores, are playful and are able to run at 40 mph for short distances. They conceive one baby which stays eight months in the mothers reversed pouch.

BUGLEWEEDS are a beautiful ground cover that has an extensive root system that is proficient and helps with preventing hillside erosion. They have an attractive purple flower that grows from rounded leaves that form mat formations in sun or partial shade in North America. As a member of the mint family it has been used medicinally for many years in treating various conditions.

BUTTERSTONE is a light green rock that is very smooth to the touch and sometimes called African Jade. It is good for grounding, healing, growth and power. An ancient stone dating to over 2500 million years ago in Southern Africa, it contains pieces of micro fossils within it. It promotes grounding earth energy and brings persistence and healing. It is said to be a connector of life energy.

**Rediscover and utilize your natural talents
in manifesting your dreams.**

NOTES

Made in the USA
San Bernardino, CA
23 June 2014